W9-AHY-524

SECRET LIVES OF
SOIL CREATURES

SECRET LIVES OF
SOIL CREATURES

SARA SWAN MILLER

Marshall Cavendish
Benchmark
New York

The author and publisher would like to thank Sidney Horenstein, Geologist and Environmental Educator Emeritus, for his generous assistance in reading the manuscript.

LIBRARY OF CONGRESS CATALOGING-IN-PUBLICATION DATA Miller, Sara Swan. Secret lives of soil creatures / by Sara Swan Miller. p. cm. — (Secret lives) Includes index. Summary: " Describes the life cycles and habits of the three kinds of animals that live in and around the soil: the decomposers, the scavengers, and the predators"—Provided by publisher. ISBN 978-0-7614-4229-5 1. Soil invertebrates—Juvenile literature. I. Title. QL365.34.M55 2010 591.75'7—dc22 2009035581

EDITOR: JOYCE STANTON   PUBLISHER: MICHELLE BISSON
ART DIRECTOR: ANAHID HAMPARIAN   SERIES DESIGNER: KRISTEN BRANCH

Photo research by Laurie Platt Winfrey, Carousel Research
Cover: Minden Pictures/ Stephen Dalton The Photographs in this book are used by permission and through the courtesy of: *Alamy:* Graham Mulroony, 8; Juniors Bildarchiv, 32; Blickwinkel, 35. *Animals/Animals:* Kathy Atkinson/OSF, 12; Robert Maier, 15; Breck Kent, 17; OSF, 20; Michael Francis Photography, 28; John Mitchell/OSF, 33. *Ardea:* Andrey Zvozkikov, 37. *Corbis:* Julie Habel, 10; Joe McDonald, 34 top; Ralph Clevenger, 43. *Getty Images:* Roy Toft, Titlepage; Terry McCormick/RF, back cover. *Minden Pictures:* Piotr Naskrecki, 8; Vincent Grafhorst, 22; Stephen Dalton, Cover & 36; Satoshi Kuribayashi, 39; Mitsuhiko Imamori, 40. *National Geographic Images:* Michael Nichols, Half title; George Grall, 18. *Photo Researchers:* Nigel Cattlin, 16; Gusto Images, 19; Larry Miller, 30; Nature's Images, 34 bottom. *Visuals Unlimited:* John Abbott, 25; John D. Cunningham, 26.

Printed in Malaysia (T)
135642

8956

Front cover: A green tiger beetle slurps up a caterpillar.

Half-title page: A banana slug in a California forest. Banana slugs have two pairs of tentacles. You can clearly see the large ones in this photo.

Title page: A banana slug feels its way along a riverbank in California.

Back cover: A giant redheaded centipede

CONTENTS

A tiny pseudoscorpion rides on a grasshopper's antenna.

LIFE IN THE SOIL

HAVE YOU EVER WONDERED ABOUT the little creatures you see moving about in the dirt? If you're like most people, you probably have no idea how many creatures are living their secret lives down in the soil. Without them, though, there would *be* no soil. And without soil, there would be no plants, no trees, and no animals on the land or in the air.

Perhaps the most important soil creatures are the **decomposers**, the little creatures that turn leaves, twigs, and fallen trees into soil. Some day in summer, go into a woodland and look up at all the leaves overhead. Now imagine all those

Who will clean up all these fallen leaves?

leaves falling to the forest floor, as they do every autumn. How deep would that layer of leaves be? Four inches (10 centimeters)? Now imagine if all those leaves just stayed on the ground all year. The next year, another layer of leaves would fall, and the next year, and the next. Imagine how deep that leaf layer would be after fifty years. If the little decomposers weren't there munching up those leaves, the woodland would be smothered. Worse yet, the nutrients in the leaves would never return to the soil. With all the nutrients trapped in leaves and no new soil being created, nothing would grow. It's a good thing there are so many earthworms, millipedes, springtails, and other **invertebrates** hard at work!

Another important group of soil creatures are the **scavengers**. Think of all the droppings that animals leave behind and all the creatures that die in the woods and fields. Imagine what the world would be like if nothing cleaned up all that waste. We're lucky to have scavengers like dung beetles to take care of all those droppings. And we should be grateful for scavengers like carrion beetles that make the bodies of dead animals disappear by eating them.

A wolf spider munches on a beetle.

Other small soil creatures are **predators**. Centipedes, wolf spiders, tiger beetles, and other predators feed mainly on invertebrates in the soil and under the leaves. All of them help keep the populations of their prey under control, so that those creatures don't become pests. In turn, the predators are food for many larger animals, from shrews to birds.

Some soil creatures are vegetarians. They eat only plant matter. Others are **omnivores**, eating both plant and animal matter. Pill bugs, for instance, feast on decaying plants, dead animals, and animal droppings. Harvestmen will eat almost anything!

How would you like to find out more about soil creatures? Let's take a closer look into their secret lives.

An earthworm
pulls a leaf down
into its burrow.

THE DECOMPOSERS

EARTHWORMS

OF ALL THE DECOMPOSERS at work in the soil, earthworms are the champions. In 1 square yard (.84 square meter) of a forest floor, there may be as many as three hundred earthworms!

Earthworms live in long, dark burrows underground. At night, they come up to the surface to feed on leaves and other plant matter. After food passes through an earthworm's digestive system, it comes out the other end as castings. The castings are rich in nutrients. Bacteria and other **micro-organisms** break down the castings and release the nutrients in a form that plants can absorb.

Earthworms do more than just help decompose leaves. By digging burrows, they bring oxygen down into the soil. Plants use the oxygen for growth. Rainwater also flows into the deep burrows, down to the roots of plants and trees. The roots absorb the water and the minerals in it so that the plants and trees can thrive.

THE SOIL MAKERS

On just 1 acre (4,047 meters) of average farmland, 16,000 pounds (7,260 kilograms) of soil pass through earthworms' guts each year and become rich castings, full of nutrients. In really wormy soil, earthworms may process 30,000 pounds (13,600 kilograms) of soil in a year.

SNAILS

Snails also help with the work of building soil. Have you ever watched a snail eat? It has a strange feeding organ called a **radula**, which is a

These garden snails have found some strawberries, one of their favorite foods.

kind of tongue covered with rows of little teeth. The snail uses its radula like a file to scrape off bits of food from plants. Muscles at the base of the radula allow the snail to move it from side to side and back and forth. A snail's radula constantly grows. When the old teeth wear down and fall off, they are replaced with new, sharp ones.

Snails like feeding on the leaves and stems of plants, including lettuce and other garden treats. It's no wonder gardeners are not at all fond of snails! But these soil creatures also eat decaying plants, so they do their part as decomposers.

Snails creep along on a single flat "foot." Muscles in the foot create a rippling movement that pushes the snail along. On the bottom of the foot is a special gland that produces a slimy **mucus** that creates a slippery track and makes travel easier. The mucus also protects a snail when it travels along sharp surfaces.

SLUGS

This hungry slug seems to be making lace.

A slug looks like a snail without a shell. Actually, many slugs do have shells, but you can't see them. They are small and hidden under the skin on the slug's back. Not having an outer shell helps the slug stretch its body out, making it slim enough to squeeze through small openings to get to its food. A slug can stretch its body far—sometimes as far as twenty times its normal length!

SECRET LIVES OF SOIL CREATURES

Like a snail, a slug has a radula to grind up its food—mostly leaves and rotting vegetation. It also moves like a snail, on a single muscular foot, and leaves a trail of mucus as it searches for its food. Slugs go out to eat at night. Their slimy trails stay on the ground for a while, allowing them to follow a trail to the same food source the next night. Other slugs will follow the trail, too. Several of them may all cluster around the same plant, grinding away. You can actually tell whether a slime trail was left by a slug or a snail. Snails leave continuous trails, but slugs' trails are broken.

A LOT OF SLUGS

There are more than forty species of slugs in the United States alone. The banana slug can be found along the West Coast, especially in California. Not all banana slugs look like bananas—yellow with brown spots. Some are green, brown, or white.

MILLIPEDES

How many segments does this millipede have?

Millipede means "thousand legs." Do these creatures really have so many legs? It may seem so at first, but no millipede has *that* many legs. A millipede's long body is made up of a series of segments, or parts. On most segments, there are two pairs of legs. Some **species** have more segments—and legs—than others. Some kinds of adult millipedes may have as many as four hundred legs. That's a lot of legs to coordinate!

Like earthworms, millipedes are important decomposers in the soil. They live under damp, dead leaves and chew up decaying vegetable matter and fungi. They can be hard to find, except at night, when they sometimes come out into the open.

Some adult millipedes **hibernate** during the winter and mate in the spring. A female may lay up to three hundred eggs. When the eggs hatch a few weeks later, out come tiny millipedes with only three pairs of legs. As the young millipedes grow, they keep adding more segments and legs.

SPRINGTAILS

Springtails have been busy down in the soil for a long time—at least 400 million years. They are such tiny creatures that you

THE LONG AND SHORT OF IT

The shortest millipede is the bristly millipede, which lives in North America and Europe. It is less than one-fifth of an inch (half a centimeter) long. Most millipedes are between 7.5 and 11 inches (19 and 28 centimeters) long. The longest ever measured was an African giant black millipede, like the one pictured above. It stretched to 15.2 inches (38.6 centimeters) and had 256 legs.

may never have noticed them. Some are microscopic, and even the largest ones are less than one-fifth of an inch (half a centimeter) long.

Springtails are everywhere! They live in just about any damp place around the world. They make their homes in mountains, fields, and forests. They even live on the surface of freshwater pools. The only place springtails can't live is below water. Wherever they live, there are plenty of them.

In 1 cubic yard (.76 cubic meter) of rich soil, there may be as many as 100,000 springtails! They feed on fungi, algae, and decaying vegetable matter.

How did springtails get their name? They can leap long distances with the help of a hinged device called a **furcula**, which is attached to their abdomen. Usually, the furcula is held in place by a kind of latch. When a springtail is startled, the latch snaps back, the furcula snaps down, and the springtail hurtles through the air. A springtail can spring a hundred times its body length. If you were 5 feet (1.5 meters) tall and could spring like a springtail, you could leap 500 feet (152 meters)! That would be amazing!

A busy dung beetle
on the move in
Botswana, Africa

THE SCAVENGERS

DUNG BEETLES

IF YOU GO OUT INTO A FARM FIELD, you may see dung beetles doing their job of cleaning up after the cows. A female dung beetle makes a ball from a cow patty and begins to roll it away. She walks backward, pushing the ball with her hind feet uphill and down. Finally, she finds a good place to store her dung ball. She lays her eggs inside the ball and buries it in the soft ground. For months, she tends the eggs

A CROWD OF DUNG BEETLES

In Africa, one scientist counted 16,000 dung beetles on a 3-pound (1.4-kilogram) elephant patty. In less than two hours, the patty was gone.

and the **grubs** that hatch from them. The tiny grubs feed on the dung ball, making it disappear.

When it comes to cleaning up animal droppings, dung beetles are the prize-winners. Hundred of beetles may attack a single pat of dung, making short work of it within a few hours or even minutes.

Some beetles don't roll their dung balls away from the dung patty. Instead, they burrow beneath it and drag the ball down into the tunnels they have made. Others just live in the dung patty itself.

CARRION BEETLES

Although dung beetles do a wonderful job of cleaning up dung, they are no help when it comes to getting rid of dead

animals. It's a good thing there are all kinds of **carrion** insects to do that job! Various flies and even wasps feed on carcasses, but carrion beetles are the real experts.

The carrion beetle's antennas point the way to a meal.

Some carrion beetles use the carcass of an animal as a place to lay their eggs. When the **larvae** hatch, they live off the rotting flesh. Burying beetles are even more helpful. They bury the carcasses. They have an excellent sense of smell, and they can detect a small dead animal from a long way away.

When a pair of male and female burying beetles smell a dead mouse, they race toward it as fast as their wings can take them. They need to find it before other carrion insects do. The beetles help each other drag the dead mouse to a good burying place where the soil is loose. They may drag the dead mouse as far as 12 feet (4 meters) before they find the right spot. Then they dig under the carcass until it is buried. After they mate on the buried body, they remove its fur. Finally, they work the body into a ball, and the female lays her eggs there.

Adult burying beetles begin to work on a dead mouse. These scavengers help keep our environment clean.

When the larvae hatch, they feed on the carcass, safe underground. The buried mouse doesn't dry out as fast as it would in the open air, and the larvae can live off the flesh for a long time. The adult beetles stay with them until they are fully developed and ready to take care of themselves. While the larvae grow, the adults feed on fly **maggots** that would otherwise compete with their young for food.

Carrion beetles live in woodlands and fields all over the world. Imagine what our environment would be like without carrion beetles and all the other scavengers to help keep it clean!

It's not hard to see how the giant red-headed centipede got its name.

THE PREDATORS

CENTIPEDES

CENTIPEDES LOOK A LOT LIKE millipedes, and these two small soil creatures are related. But if you look closely, you can tell them apart. Although both have long, segmented bodies, millipedes have two pairs of legs on each segment, while centipedes have just one pair per segment. A centipede's legs are much longer than a millipede's, and it can speed along at quite a clip.

A giant redheaded centipede devours a wolf spider. This kind of centipede can grow to nearly 8 inches (20 centimeters) long.

Centipedes need to be fast, because they have to chase after their prey. They eat mostly insects, spiders, and earthworms. Big ones like the Texas giant centipede even hunt birds, toads, lizards, and mice. Although centipedes are nearly blind, they can search out their prey by using their sensitive **antennas** and by feeling vibrations in the ground.

Right under a centipede's head are a pair of poison claws. These claws, which act more like jaws, have developed over

tens of millions of years from what once was a pair of walking legs. A centipede grips its prey with its claws and injects a powerful **venom**, which quickly kills the victim. Then the centipede can gobble up its dinner.

A REALLY BIG CENTIPEDE!

Centipedes live all over the world, in all kinds of habitats where there is a bit of moisture. Most are fairly small, but one species in Central America can grow to be 12 inches (30.5 centimeters) long. You wouldn't want to be bitten by that!

PSEUDOSCORPIONS

The next time you go into the woods, take along a magnifying glass. If you look carefully under the leaves, you may see tiny creatures that look like miniature scorpions scurrying around. Like scorpions, they can run backward, sideways, and forward. Will they sting like scorpions?

No, these scorpion look-alikes are perfectly harmless. Pseudoscorpions, or "false scorpions," don't have a stinging tail like true scorpions. But they do have a pair of large pincerlike claws called pedipalps just behind their head,

A house pseudo-scorpion hunts for book lice.

and the pedipalps have venom glands. Pseudoscorpions won't use their venom on people, though, only on their insect prey. They attack all kinds of insects, including ants, mites, and small flies. Inside a house, they may feed on the larvae of clothes moths and on book lice, so be grateful if you see them indoors!

WOLF SPIDERS

Wolf spiders are also fierce predators. A hungry wolf spider hides in the leaves on the dark forest floor. It waits in ambush for a tasty insect to happen by. If it spots a beetle, it leaps and grabs its prey with its sharp fangs. As the spider bites, it injects venom into the struggling insect. The beetle quickly dies, and the wolf spider chews its victim to a pulp

SECRET LIVES OF SOIL CREATURES

and sucks up the juices. Then it settles down to wait for its next meal to come along.

People gave the wolf spider its name because it is a fearsome hunter, like a wolf. With its eight eyes, the wolf spider has good vision, which helps it both spot prey and avoid predators. Its eight eyes are arranged in three rows. On the bottom row are four small eyes. Two of these point forward and two point to the side. On the top row are two large forward-pointing eyes. Two other large eyes, located on each side of the body in the middle row, point upward.

After a pair of wolf spiders mate, the female spins a sheet of silk, lays her eggs in the middle, shapes the silk into a sac, and covers the sac with a final layer of silk. She attaches the

Wolf spiders can catch big insects.

Top: A female wolf spider carries her egg sac about for weeks.
Bottom: After the spiderlings hatch, they climb aboard their mother and stay with her a bit longer.

sac to the end of her abdomen and carts it around for several weeks. Finally, she opens the sac with her jaws, and masses of spiderlings come out. There may be as many as two hundred of them! They all climb onto the top of their mother's abdomen, and she carries them around for another week. After that, they have to fend for themselves.

HISTER BEETLES

When an animal dies in the woods, hister beetles are usually the first insects on the scene. Most of them are not there to eat the carrion, however. They're more interested in eating the carrion-eating insects that arrive next.

During the day, some hister beetles hide under the dead animal. When night falls, they dig inside the corpse in search

SECRET LIVES OF SOIL CREATURES

of maggots, especially blowfly maggots. They seize their prey with their sharp, curved jaws and slice it up. They also eat any **pupae** they find.

After mating, the females lay their eggs in the corpse. As soon as the larvae hatch, they start devouring blowfly maggots. The beetle larvae don't have much time to reach adulthood, because their food supply won't last long. They go through only two larval stages. By the time the carrion rots away and the maggots are gone, the hister beetles have usually grown up. Now they can go off to find fresh carrion.

A hister beetle sits on the feathers of a dead bird, waiting for its prey to come along.

It's not hard to identify hister beetles. Most have rounded bodies that are shiny black, metallic green, or bronze, and their heads are tucked down. They look like tiny six-legged turtles roving about the forest floor. They act a bit like turtles, too. When a hister beetle is threatened, it may pull its head, legs, and antennas into its shell and hold perfectly still until the danger has passed.

TIGER BEETLES

Tiger beetles are predators, too. How did they get their name? For one thing, many have striped markings that make them look a bit like tigers. The real reason, though, is that they are fierce hunters. A sand tiger beetle can kill and eat insects and spiders much bigger than itself.

Tiger beetles run swiftly on their long legs. They can speed along at up to 5 miles (8 kilometers) an hour. They have big eyes that help them focus on their prey and huge, strong

A tiger beetle's jaws are huge. This fierce predator has captured a caterpillar.

SECRET LIVES OF SOIL CREATURES

jaws for grabbing and crunching their meal. When a tiger beetle catches an insect, it spits out digestive juices that start turning its victim into mush. Then the tiger beetle can chew on the softened flesh and suck up the juices.

Even tiger beetle grubs are fierce predators. As soon as a grub hatches, it digs a tunnel, loosening the soil with its powerful jaws and digging away with its shovel-like head. Usually, the grub hides just inside the entrance to its tunnel. When another insect happens along, the grub makes a grab for it and starts pulling it down into the tunnel. The grub has little hooks on its body that help it hang on to the tunnel walls. No matter how much its prey struggles, the tiger beetle grub keeps its grip until the insect is exhausted. Then the grub gobbles up its meal.

Tiger beetles are fast fliers.

Ground Beetles

Most ground beetles are predators, but they are also good at defending themselves. Like other beetles, they have hard shells that are not at all easy for an enemy to bite through. And like other beetles, the ground beetle has a pair of hard front wings that form a protective cover for its body.

While all beetles have ways to protect themselves, the bombardier beetle has the best defense of all. When this ground beetle is startled—by a toad, for instance—it lifts its tail and with a *pop!* squirts out a hot, stinging mixture of chemicals. As the toad struggles to get the irritating spray out of its eyes, the bombardier swiftly escapes on its long, spindly legs.

The bombardier beetle has excellent aim. It can curl its "hoses" to point in any direction. If an ant bites anywhere on its body, the beetle knows just where to aim its spray. It always repels the ant, because the bombardier never misses!

The bombardier is a fierce predator. During the day, it

SECRET LIVES OF SOIL CREATURES

hides under rocks. At night, it runs about chasing down its Bombs away! prey. With its large **compound eyes**, it has excellent vision. It can even see in color. Bombardier beetles like to eat any soft-bodied creature, from caterpillars to maggots to slugs and snails. Gardeners appreciate these beetles because the bombardiers feed on many garden pests.

These baby pill bugs have just come out of their mother's pouch.

SOME INTERESTING
OMNIVORES

PILL BUGS

ON THE FOREST FLOOR LURK the pill bugs. They are sometimes called sow bugs or wood lice, but they aren't really bugs *or* lice. They are crustaceans, animals related to lobsters and crabs. They can only live in moist places because they need to keep their gills wet in order to breathe. They also lose water easily through their skin and can dry out quickly in the sun. Pill bugs usually hide beneath damp leaves, under rocks, or in decaying logs.

Do you know why they are called pill bugs? If one of these little soil creatures is threatened, it curls up into a tight ball that looks like a pill. Curling up protects the animal's soft underbelly from predators. A pill bug has many enemies. Frogs, toads, newts, and small mammals like shrews all enjoy the taste of pill bugs. Spiders are another threat. They inject venom into a pill bug's body and then suck up the juices.

Pill bugs are omnivores, eating both animal and vegetable matter. Their favorite food is decaying wood and plants. Like earthworms and other decomposers, they digest the food and release the nutrients back into the soil. Pill bugs also help clean up the environment by eating dead animals and animal droppings.

HARVESTMEN

Harvestmen, often called daddy longlegs, are also omnivores. They are strange-looking creatures. They have small round bodies and incredibly long bent legs. Their pill-like bodies are

held suspended just above the ground by their skinny legs.

Harvestmen belong to a group of animals called Opiliones (oh-pill-ee-OH-naze), which means "shepherd creatures." The Opiliones don't act like shepherds, though. They got their name because a long time ago shepherds walked about on stilts to watch over their flocks. The Opiliones look like they are walking on stilts, too.

Harvestmen usually live in damp forests under leaf litter. They creep about on their spindly legs searching for small

A harvest-man seems to walk on stilts.

HARVESTTIME

Harvestmen got their name because farmers often saw them in late summer and fall, at harvesttime. The men thought that the odd-looking creatures were also harvesting food for the winter.

insects, fungi, dead animals, and rotting vegetation. Although they have only two eyes, they have good vision. Hairs on their legs also help them sense food. They grab their meal with their claws, grind it up, and suck it into their stomachs.

Although they are related to spiders, harvestmen have no fangs or venom glands. A harvestman will never bite you, even if you pick it up. Those long legs do tickle, though!

Isn't it amazing how many soil creatures there are? If you get down on your hands and knees and really look at the ground, maybe you can discover even more.

SECRET LIVES OF SOIL CREATURES

Words to Know

antennas The long, thin body parts on the heads of some creatures, such as insects, that are used to sense touch or smells. Antennas come in pairs.

carrion Dead and rotting flesh. Carrion insects feed on dead animals.

compound eye An eye made up of thousands of separate units that work together to form an image. Bombardier beetles and many other insects have compound eyes.

decomposers Creatures that feed on dead plant and animal matter and release the nutrients into the soil.

furcula A hingelike structure under a springtail's body that helps it spring into the air.

grub The larva of a beetle. In this early stage of growth, the insect looks like a worm.

hibernate To spend the winter in an inactive, sleeplike state.

invertebrate An animal that does not have a backbone.

larva (*plural,* **larvae**) The newly hatched form of some insects and other invertebrates. A larva has a soft, wingless body that looks like a worm. A caterpillar, for example, is the larva of a moth or butterfly.

maggots The larvae of some insects, such as flies.

microorganisms Living things that are too small to be seen with the naked eye.

mucus A slimy fluid that protects parts of an animal's body. In humans, for example, mucus coats and protects the insides of the mouth, nose, and throat.

omnivore A creature that eats both animals and plants.

predators Animals that live by hunting other animals for food.

pupa (*plural,* **pupae**) The next stage of development for an insect after being a larva, before it becomes an adult.

radula A tonguelike organ covered with rows of little teeth, which snails, slugs, and some other animals use to eat.

scavengers Animals that feed on dead animals or on animal droppings.

species A group of animals or plants that have many characteristics in common. Members of the same species can mate and bear offspring.

venom The poison of some spiders, snakes, and other animals.

Learning More

BOOKS

Blaxland, Beth. *Centipedes, Millipedes, and Their Relatives: Myriapods.* Broomall, PA: Chelsea House, 2003.

Dixon, Norma. *Lowdown on Earthworms.* Markham, ON: Fitzhenry and Whiteside, 2005.

Halfmann, Janet. *Life under a Stone.* Mankato, MN: Creative Education, 2001.

Merrick, Patrick. *Centipedes.* Chanhassen, MN: Child's World, 2003.

INTERNET SITES

Insect Theme Page

http://enchantedlearning.com/themes/insects.shtml

The *Insect Theme Page* has lots of insect activities, including crafts, printable books and coloring books, drawing worksheets, and word games.

Yucky Worm World

http://yucky.discovery.com/flash/worm/

Learn all about earthworms and their role as "nature's recyclers." This site offers interesting information as well as experiments, crafts, and other activities.

Index

Page numbers for illustrations are in boldface

About the Author

SARA SWAN MILLER has written more than sixty books for young people. She has enjoyed working with children all her life, first as a Montessori nursery-school teacher and later as an outdoor environmental educator at the Mohonk Preserve in New Paltz, New York. The best part of her work is helping kids appreciate the beauty of the natural world.